Reward Stickers

1) Most of the activities in this book should be at an appropriate developmental level, which will allow your child to do them independently. But don't hesitate to help them! When parents are involved in the learning process, it increases a child's intellectual curiosity and creates a more effective, supportive learning environment.

2) To support your child's learning, review the **"To Parents"** section featured below the instructions. These tips offer parents effective ways to explain the activity to your child.

3) As mentioned on the previous page, this book is divided into three steps. Depending on the ability of your child, start with pages that they can handle and work up to the more difficult ones after a while. Some activities return to an earlier level of difficulty, and these will help strengthen your child's scissor-handling skills. If your child still has difficulty using the scissors, you can show them how to use the scissors by example.

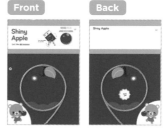

Another feature of this book is that you can enjoy the illustrations on the back side of the pages. The back side of each page also has pictures, cutting lines, and starting marks for the scissors, so if your child is left-handed, they can look at the pictures on the back side and cut.

4) In order to handle scissors safely, it is important for parents and children to share the following rules: (1) Tell an adult before using scissors; (2) Always use scissors while sitting; (3) Don't use the scissors to point; (4) Don't cut anyone's hair, including your own or your pet's; (5) Hand the scissors to an adult when you are done using them.

5) When your child finishes each activity, let them choose a **reward sticker** to place on the page. Be sure to praise your child's good work! Be specific with your praise, saying something like, "You did a good job!" or "You were very patient!"

How to Hold Scissors

Insert your thumb into the smaller opening of the scissors. Then insert your index finger and middle finger (in some cases, your ring finger as well) into the larger opening.

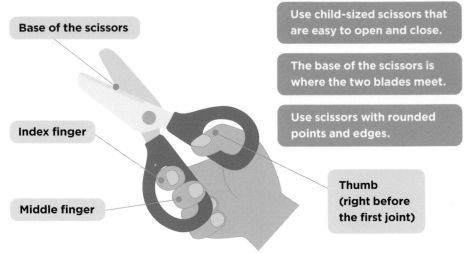

Base of the scissors

Use child-sized scissors that are easy to open and close.

The base of the scissors is where the two blades meet.

Use scissors with rounded points and edges.

Index finger

Middle finger

Thumb
(right before
the first joint)

How to Use Scissors

When using scissors, the elbow of the arm holding the scissors should be touching the body at the waist. Scissors should be held straight out from the body, and the paper should be held perpendicular to the scissors.

Hold the scissors in one hand and the paper in the other hand. Initially, it may be necessary for a parent to hold the paper.

Insert the paper deep into the scissors. Open and partially close the blades repeatedly to cut a straight line.

Caution: The paper in this book can be sharp. Take care when handling. This book contains small stickers. Keep out of mouths. Be careful when using scissors, and use them only with an adult.

Water the Flowers

Cut the ▨▨▨▨▨ into several pieces.
Put them on the picture to water the flowers.

To Parents | While your child is getting used to cutting with scissors, place your hand over their hand to help guide them. Let them cut one "water" piece at a time while saying, "Let's water the flowers."

Parents: Cut this line for your child.

Water the Flowers

Parents: Cut the pink line. Your child can complete the rest of the activity.

4

Cut the water into several pieces.

Put the pieces on the picture to water the flowers.

Good job!

Flapping Penguin

Example

Cut the ✂ and fold on the ········ to flap the penguin's wings.

Flapping Penguin
Tips for cutting horizontal lines.

It is difficult to use scissors to cut in a horizontal way.

Turn the paper so you can cut the line going straight out in front of you.

Peeka...

boo!

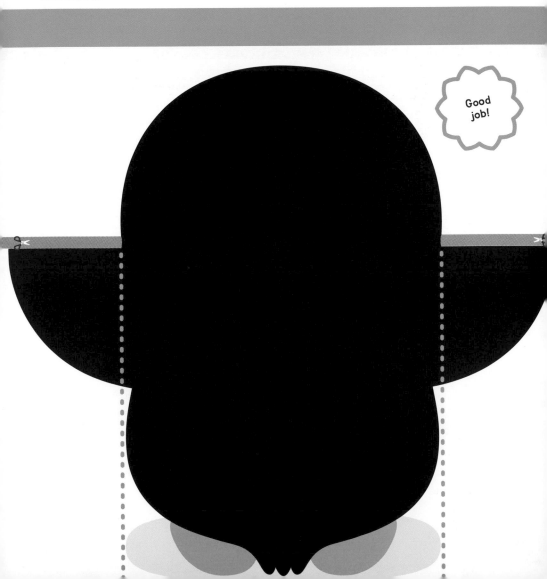

Good job!

Play the Drums

Cut the ✂ ▬▬▬▬ and fold on the ∙ ∙ ∙ ∙ ∙ ∙ ∙ ∙
to play the drums.

To Parents Cut the thick pink line first. Encourage your child to cut the two gray lines and fold on the dotted lines. Then let them make the cat play the drums.

Parents: Cut this line for your child.

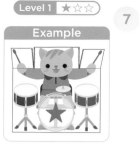

Example

Play the Drums

Parents: Cut the pink line. Your child can complete the rest of the activity.

Turn the paper so your child can cut the gray lines vertically.

Rat-a-tat!

Good job!

Strawberry Cake

Cut out the pieces on the  along the ✂.
Put the strawberries on the cake.

Example

Parents: Cut this line for your child.

Strawberry Cake

Parents: Cut the pink line. Your child can complete the rest of the activity.

Cut out each strawberry.

Put the strawberries on the cake.

Good job!

Play with Butterflies

Cut out the pieces on the  along the ✂.
Put the butterflies on the picture and let them fly.

Example

Cut the pieces along the scissors. Put the butterflies on the picture and let them fly.

Parents: Cut this line for your child.

Play with Butterflies

Parents: Cut the pink line. Your child can complete the rest of the activity.

12

Cut out each butterfly.

Put the butterflies on the picture.

Good job!

Sea Animals

Cut out the pieces on the  along the ✂. Put the animals on the picture and let them swim.

Parents: Cut this line for your child.

Sea Animals

Parents: Cut the pink line. Your child can complete the rest of the activity.

14

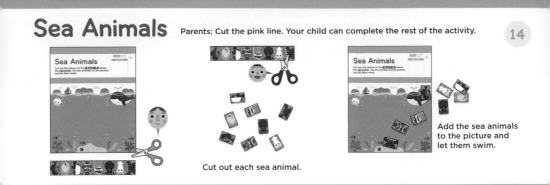

Cut out each sea animal.

Add the sea animals to the picture and let them swim.

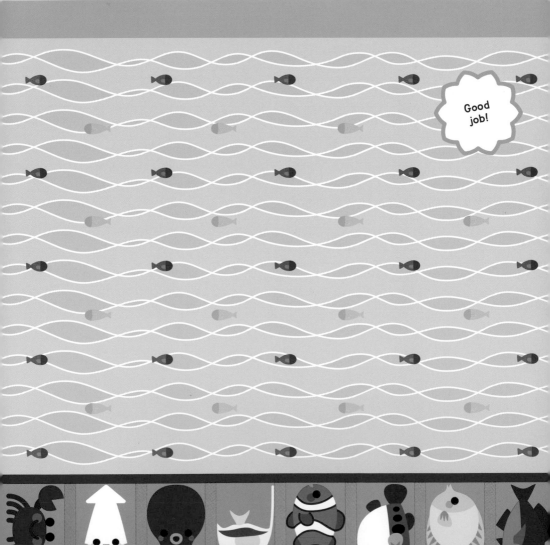

Good job!

Elephant
Shower

Example

Cut the ✂ ━━━━ and fold on the • • • • • • •
to watch the elephant splash the kids.

To Parents	Have your child practice cutting short lines. Your child should keep the scissors open and close them only slightly to make the cuts at the base of the scissors, without closing the scissors all the way.

Elephant Shower

Tips for cutting longer lines.

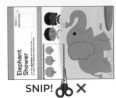

SNIP!

Don't completely close the scissors in the middle of the line.

Close the scissors only halfway while cutting the line.

Reopen the scissors wide and continue cutting.

Fold the paper and watch the elephant splash the kids.

Good job!

Ice Cream Scoops

Cut the ✂ and fold on the · · · · · · · ·
to put ice cream on the cone.

Example

Ice Cream Scoops

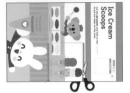

Cut the gray line. Don't completely close the scissors while cutting.

Fold the paper to add ice cream scoops.

Here is your ice cream cone!

Good job!

Swinging Panda

Cut the  and fold on the •••••••• to see the baby panda swing in a tire.

To Parents | After your child cuts the paper and folds on the dotted line, say "Swing, swing!" while closing and opening the paper.

Example

Swinging Panda

Watch the playful
baby panda swing
in the tire.

Good
job!

Cat Ears

Example

Cut the  to give the cat ears.

Cat Ears

Make different cats by changing the positions of the ears.

To Parents | When your child places the triangles on the cat's head, let them know there are different ways to place them.

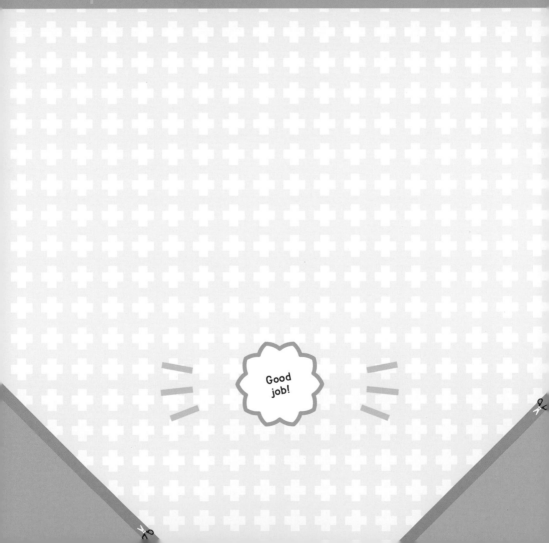

Good job!

House Puzzle

Cut the  and match the pieces to make a window on the house.

To Parents When your child is cutting a diagonal line, have them hold the paper close to the line with the hand that isn't holding the scissors. This will prevent the paper from shifting.

Parents: Cut this line for your child.

House Puzzle

Parents: Cut the pink line. Your child can complete the rest of the activity.

24

Match the puzzle pieces to make a window.

Good job!

Bus Windows

Cut the ✂ and put a friend in each window of the bus.

Example

To Parents | This activity practices cutting from two different directions to make a square. Ask your child to cut to where the lines cross.

Bus Windows

Tips for cutting corners.

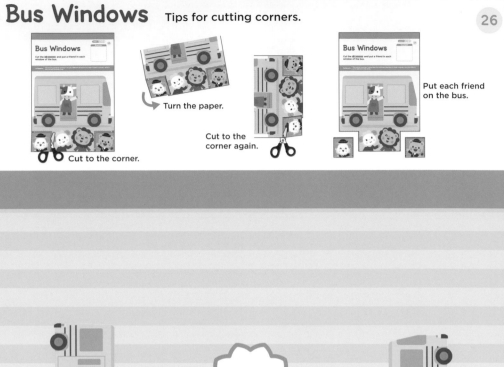

Cut to the corner.

Turn the paper.

Cut to the corner again.

Put each friend on the bus.

Good job!

Toy Box

Cut the  and fold on the ········· to make a toy box.

Parents: Cut this line for your child.

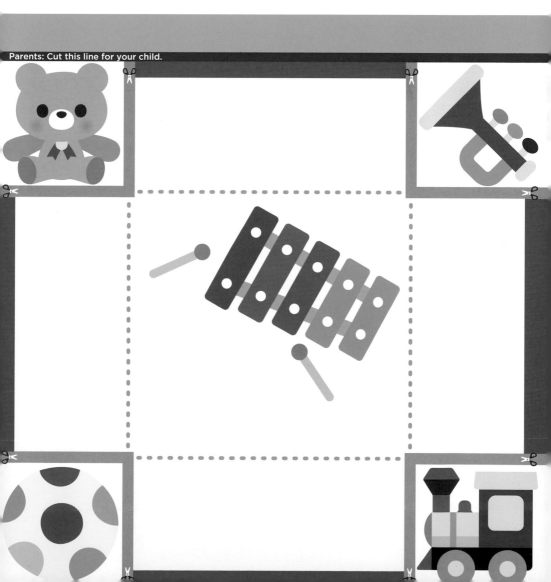

Toy Box

Parents: Cut the pink line. Your child can complete the rest of the activity.

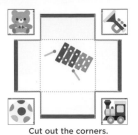

Cut out the corners.

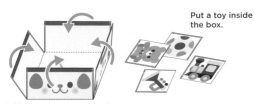

Fold the paper to make a box.

Put a toy inside the box.

Good job!

Gentle Elephant

Cut the ✂ to make the elephant's trunk and legs swing.

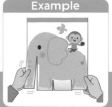
To Parents | Have your child practice cutting short and long lines. Your child should keep the scissors open and close them only slightly to make the cuts at the base of the scissors, without closing the scissors all the way.

Watermelon Puzzle

Cut the ✂ and combine the two pieces to make a round watermelon.

To Parents | Your child can practice cutting long lines, which requires them to open and partially close the scissors repeatedly. But if your child has difficulty, cut halfway for them and let them cut the rest.

Watermelon Puzzle

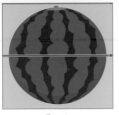

Front

Back

Pretend to eat the juicy watermelon.

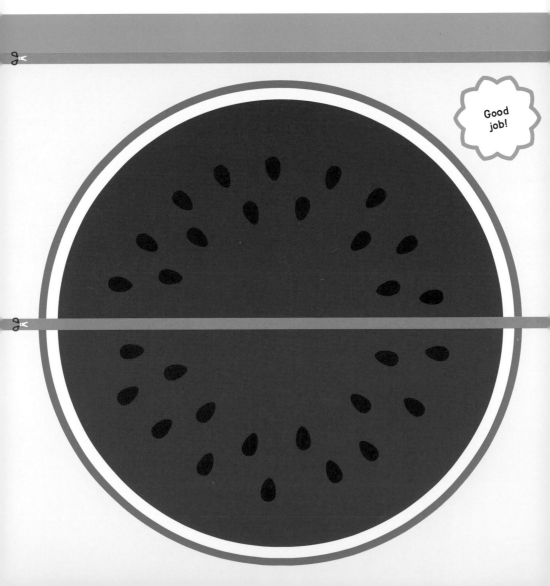

Good job!

Tower Puzzle

Cut the 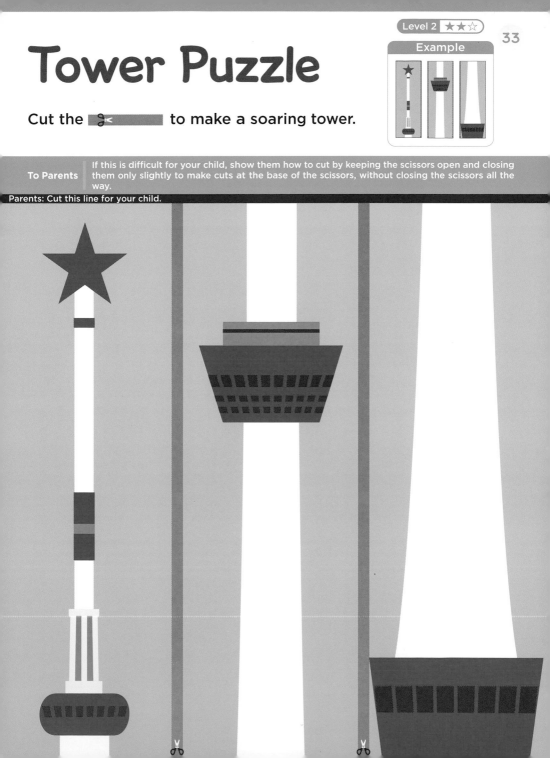 to make a soaring tower.

Example

To Parents If this is difficult for your child, show them how to cut by keeping the scissors open and closing them only slightly to make cuts at the base of the scissors, without closing the scissors all the way.

Parents: Cut this line for your child.

Tower Puzzle

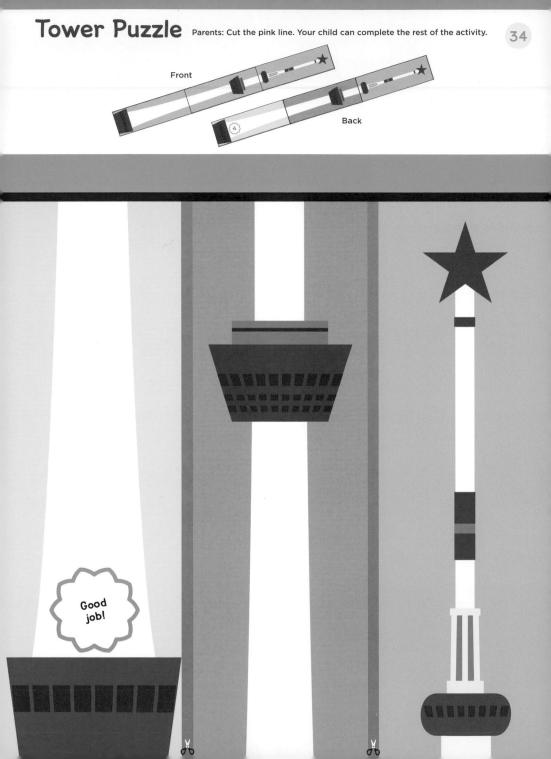

Parents: Cut the pink line. Your child can complete the rest of the activity.

34

Front

Back

Good job!

Melon Puzzle

Cut the  and combine the three pieces to make a picture.

| To Parents | For this activity, your child will form a picture with the three puzzle pieces. Both sides of the pieces are identical, so either side may be used to complete the puzzle. |

Parents: Cut this line for your child.

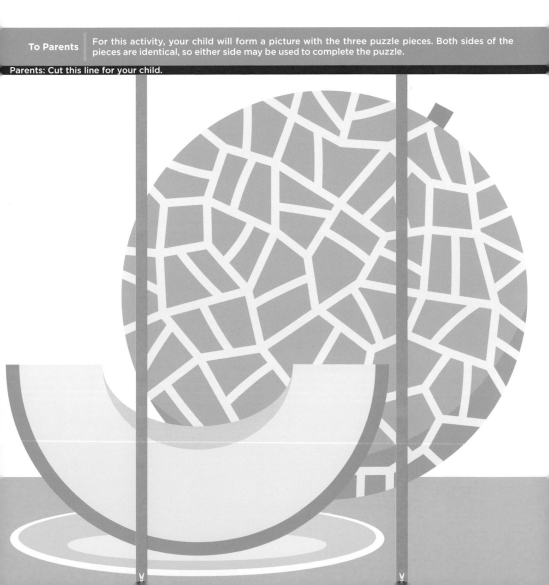

Melon Puzzle

Parents: Cut the pink line. Your child can complete the rest of the activity.

36

Front

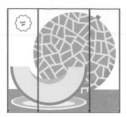

Back

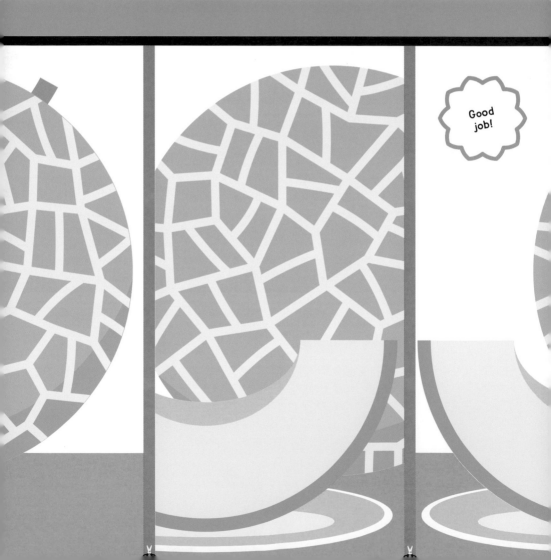

Good job!

Train Puzzle

Example

Cut the ✂ and combine the three pieces to make a speedy train.

To Parents In this activity, your child can line up the three puzzle pieces to form a long train. The pieces on the back side of this page can be rearranged to form a different train.

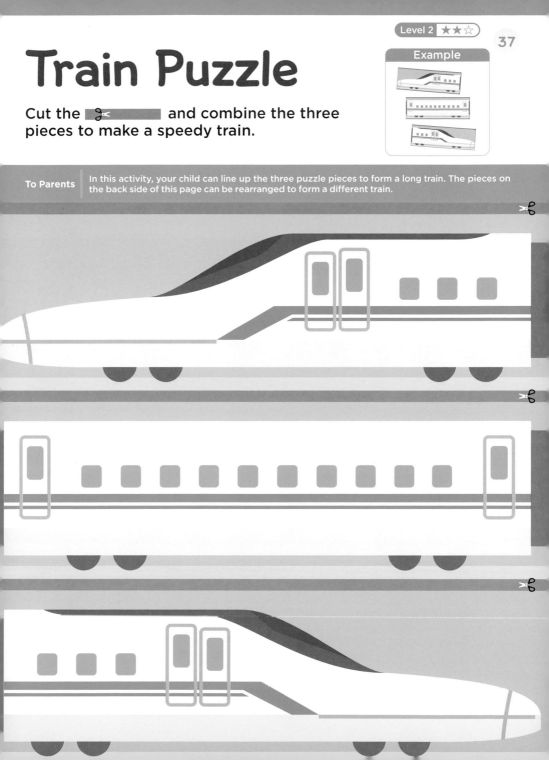

Train Puzzle

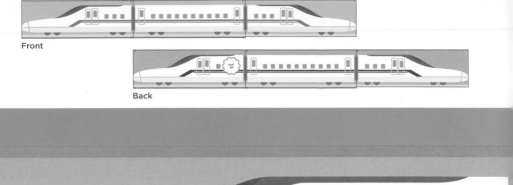

Front

Back

Good
job!

Hot Pizza

Cut the ✂ and combine the four pieces to make a round pizza.

Example

Hot Pizza

Parents: Cut the pink line. Your child can complete the rest of the activity.

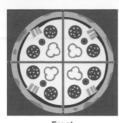

Front

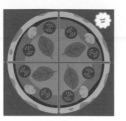

Back

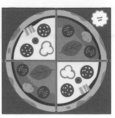

Combination

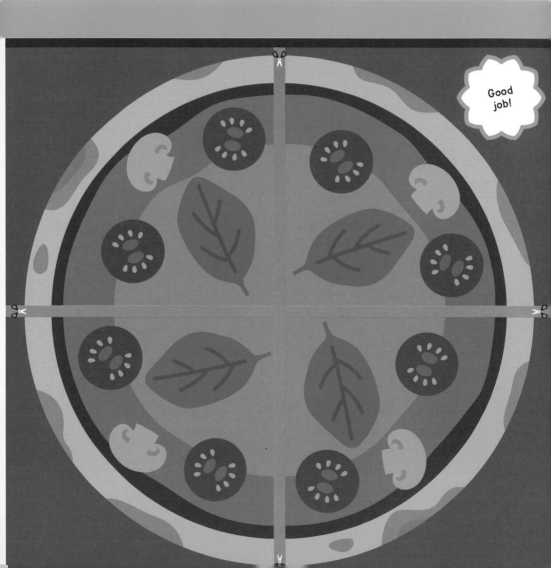

Juicy Watermelon

Example

Cut the ✂━━━ .

To Parents | Curved lines should be cut by turning the paper to keep the line vertical to your body, not by moving the scissors in the direction of the line. Show your child an example.

Turn the paper.

Hold scissors straight in front of you, and move them calmly and slowly.

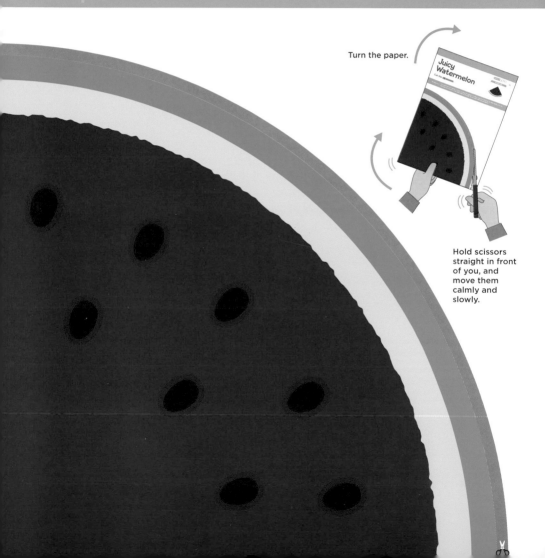

Pretend to eat a juicy slice of watermelon.

Good job!

Yellow Bananas

Example

Cut the .

Mighty Dinosaur

Example

Cut the ✂ ▬▬▬.

| To Parents | This activity focuses on cutting a reverse S-shape line. As this can be difficult, encourage your child to cut a little at a time while slowly shifting the position of the paper. |

Good job!

Wiggly Octopus

Cut the ✂ .

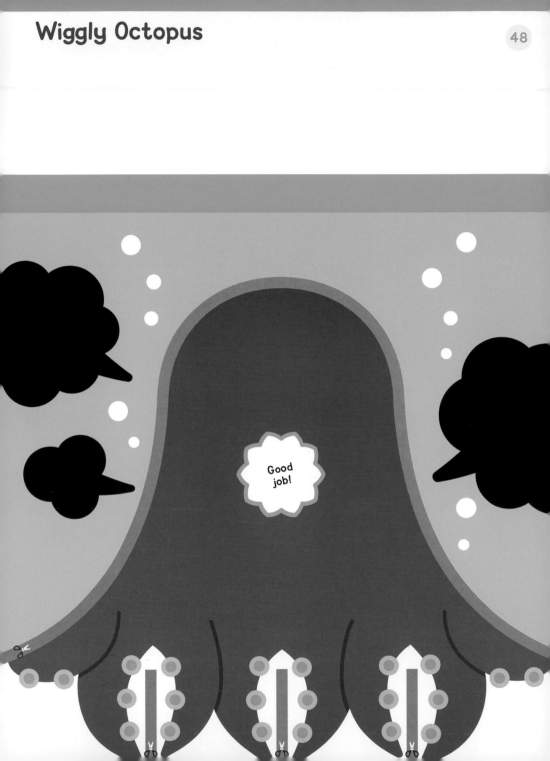

Colorful Umbrella

Cut the ✂ ▬▬ .

Car Ride

Cut the 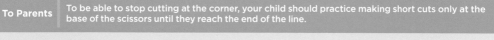.

Example

To Parents | To be able to stop cutting at the corner, your child should practice making short cuts only at the base of the scissors until they reach the end of the line.

Car Ride

King's Crown

Cut the ✂ ▬▬▬▬ .

Example

To Parents | Once your child is comfortable with the scissors, let them try to do it without your help. When they are able to do it on their own, praise them for a job well done.

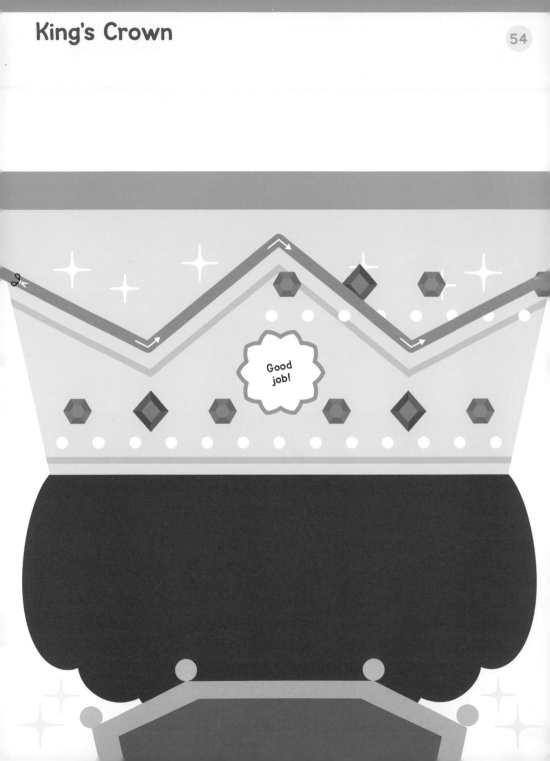

Blue Bird

Cut the .

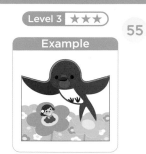

Example

Happy Bunny

Cut the .

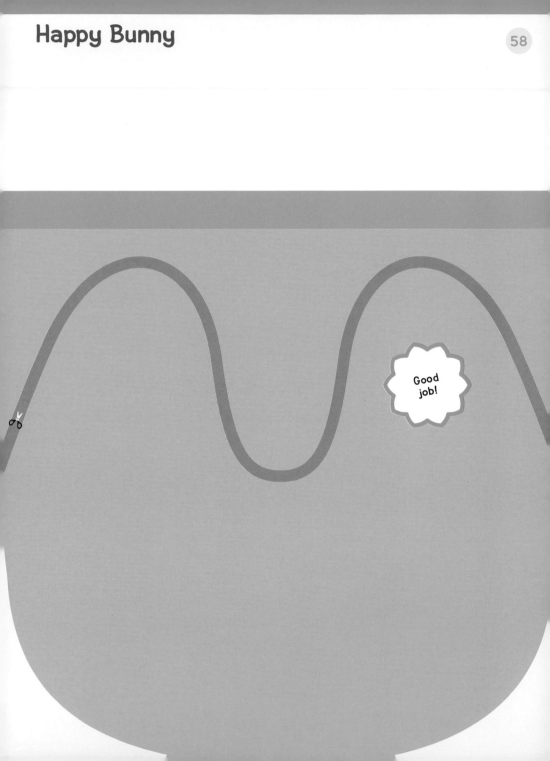

Flying Butterfly

Cut the ✂ ▬▬▬ and make the butterfly flutter.

To Parents When your child gets to a corner, let them turn the paper around and start cutting again. Show them where to stop cutting so you can shift the paper.

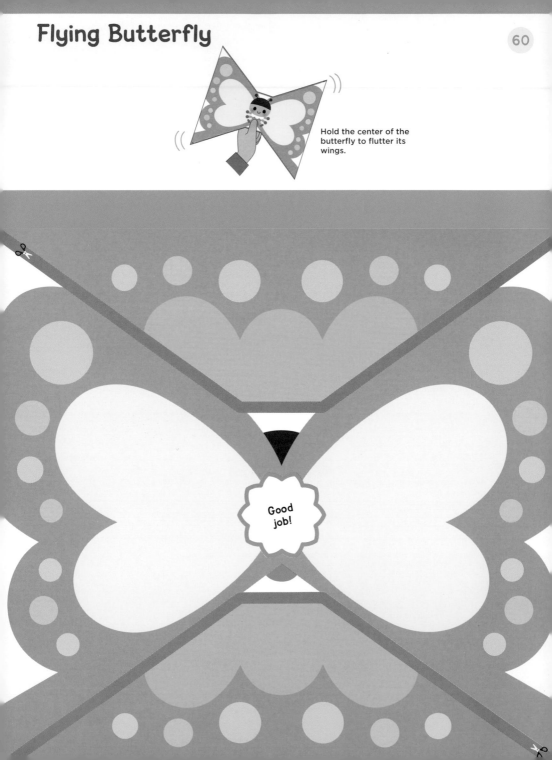

Hold the center of the butterfly to flutter its wings.

Good job!

Shiny
Apple

Cut the ✂ ▬▬▬▬ .

Turn the paper
as you cut.

Example

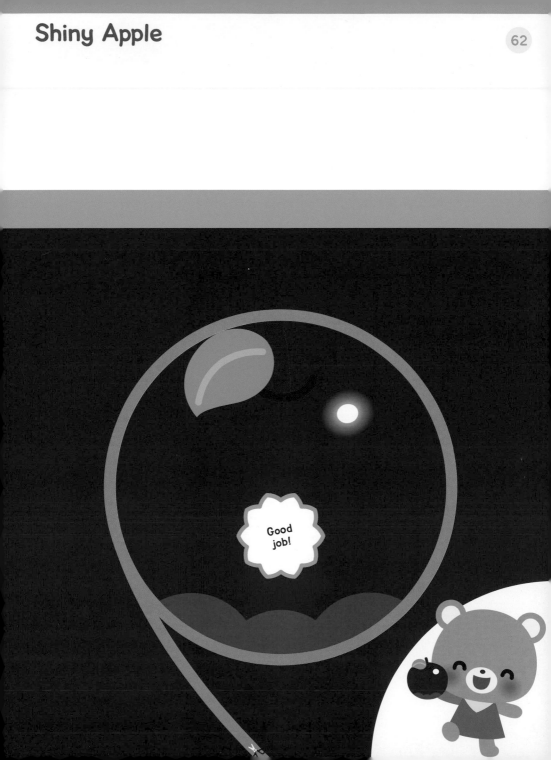

Swimming Dolphin

Example

Cut the ✂ and fold on the ········· to make the dolphin swim.

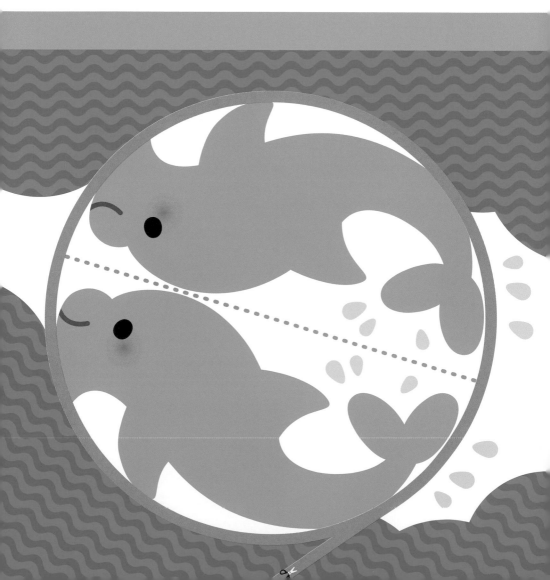

Good
job!

Walking Dog

Cut the  and make the dog walk.

Example

Good job!

Toy Closet

Cut the ✂ and fold on the • • • • • • • •
to open and close the closet doors.

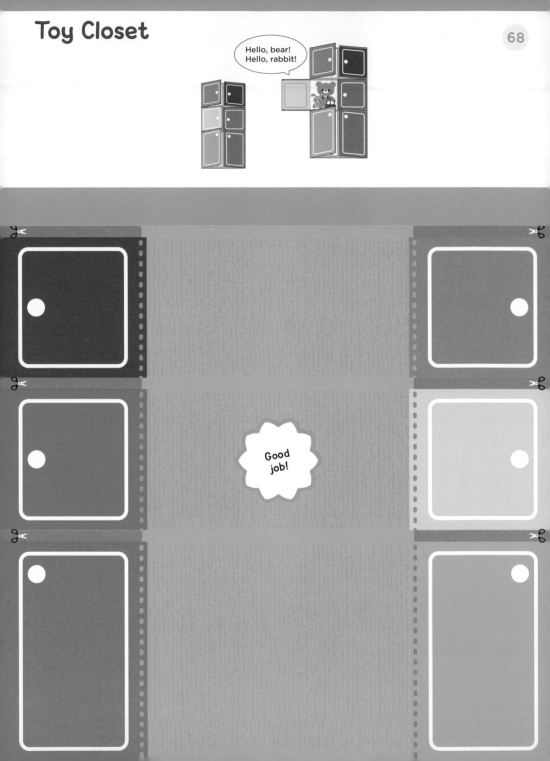

Apple Tree

Cut out the pieces on the ●●●●●● along the ✂ . Put apples on the tree.

To Parents	Cut the pink line and then hand the strip of paper to your child. Have your child hold it in one hand and cut off each piece, starting from the side with the scissors.

Parents: Cut this line for your child.

Apple Tree

Parents: Cut the pink line. Your child can complete the rest of the activity.

70

Cut out the apples.

Put the apples
on the tree.

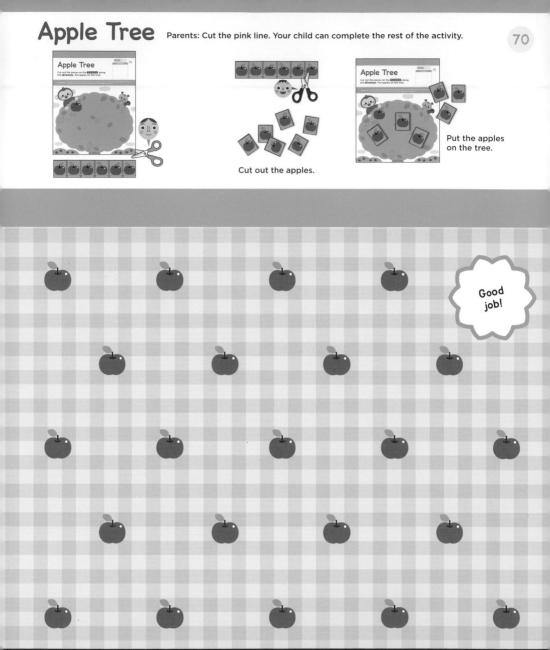

Good
job!

Flower Garden

Cut out the pieces on the ▨▨▨▨▨ along the ✂━━━━ . Put flowers in the garden.

Example
Flower Garden

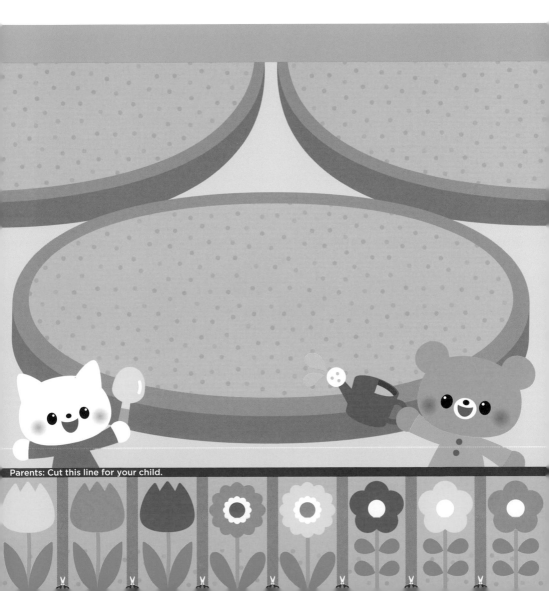

Parents: Cut this line for your child.

Flower Garden

Parents: Cut the pink line. Your child can complete the rest of the activity.

72

Cut out the flowers.

Put the flowers in the garden.

Good job!

Reach High

Cut the ✂ and fold on the • • • • • • • •.
Then fold each flap up.

To Parents When the paper is cut and folded, your child can enjoy changing the picture. When the picture is changed, say to your child, "The hat blew off!" or "The dinosaur saved the hat!"

Example

Pink Pig

Cut the and put the pig's ears, nose, and mouth on the face.

Example

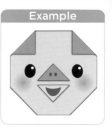

Pink Pig

Parents: Cut the pink line. Your child can complete the rest of the activity.

76

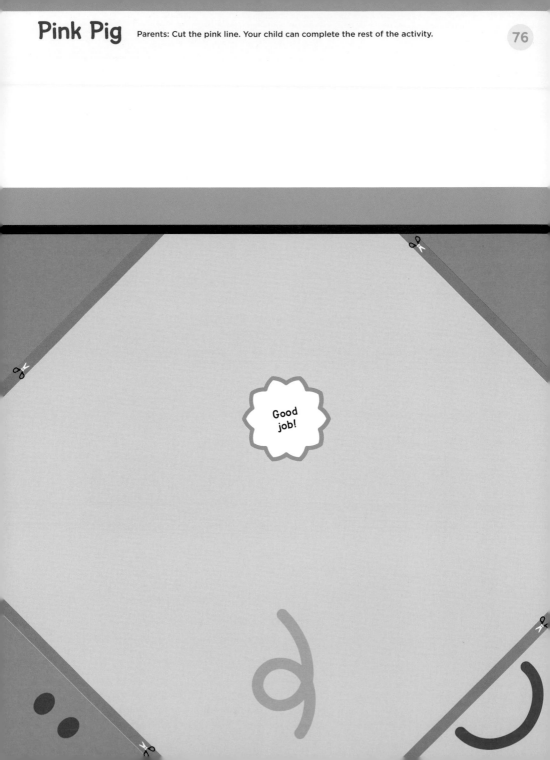

Kitchen Table

Cut the and fold the paper on the •••••••• to add food to the table.

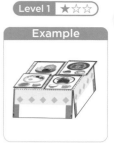

Parents: Cut this line for your child.

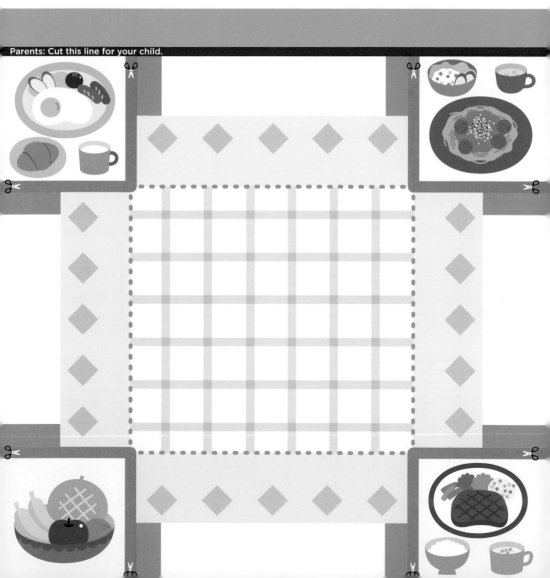

Kitchen Table

Parents: Cut the pink line. Your child can complete the rest of the activity.

78

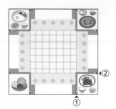

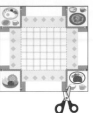

Cut each corner from opposite directions.

Cut each line to the corner. Turn the paper and cut the other line to the corner.

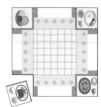

Put the food on the table.

Good job!

Get Dressed

Example

Cut the  to put clothes on the boy and girl.

To Parents This activity focuses on cutting short horizontal and vertical lines. Your child's scissors should always be pointed away from the body. Have them cut a vertical line, then turn the paper so the next line being cut is vertical, and cut to where the first one ended.

Get Dressed
Tips for cutting individual pieces.

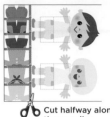

Cut halfway along the gray line.

Turn the paper, then cut to where the last cut ended.

Put the clothes on the kids.

Good job!

Elephant and Giraffe

Cut the 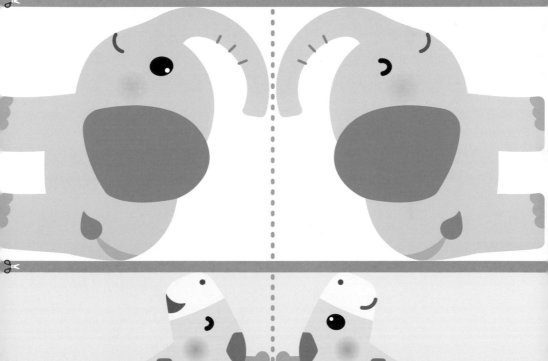 and fold on the • • • • • • • •
to make the elephant and giraffe stand.

Example

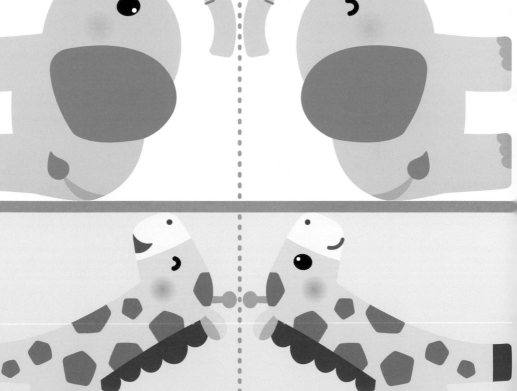

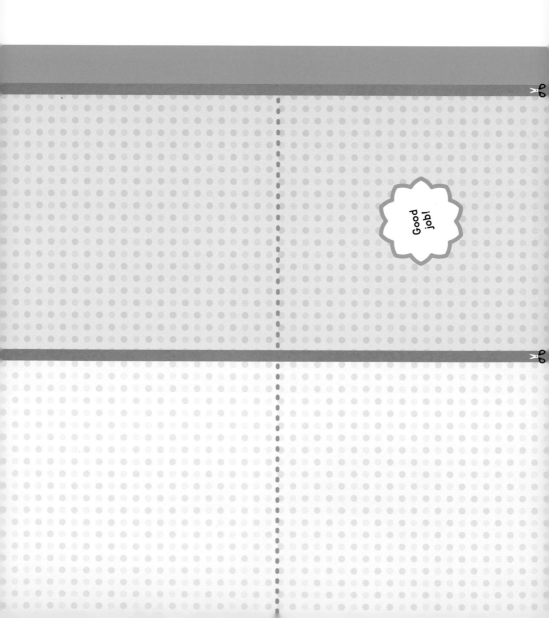

Good job!

Sled Race

First cut the .
Then cut the .
Fold the paper on the • • • • • • • • to
make the sleds stand.

Fold

Example

To Parents This activity practices cutting to the end of the line without cutting off the paper. When your child is close to the end of the line, have them cut a little at a time, stopping at the right position.

Parents: Cut this line for your child.

Sled Race

Parents: Cut the pink line. Your child can complete the rest of the activity.

84

Place the finished work on the desk and try to move it by blowing.

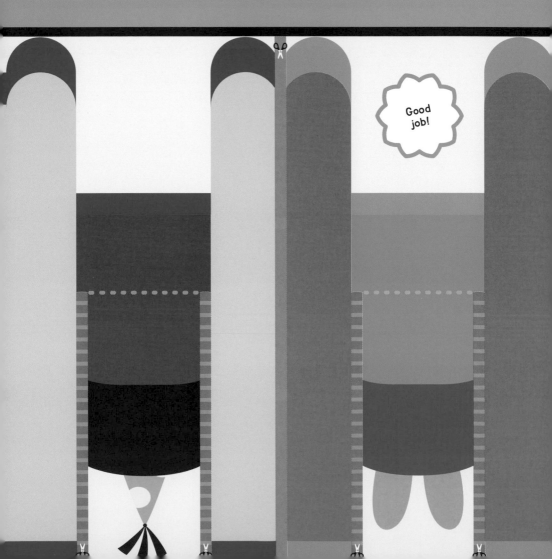

Good job!

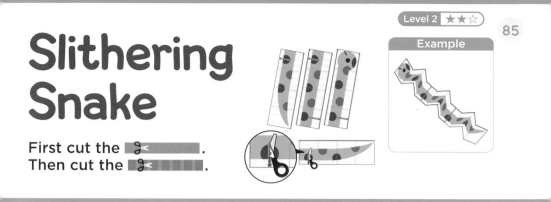

Slithering Snake

Example

First cut the ✂ ▬▬▬▬▬ .
Then cut the ✂ ▬▬▬▬▬ .

To Parents | Show your child how to fold the paper in a zigzag pattern.

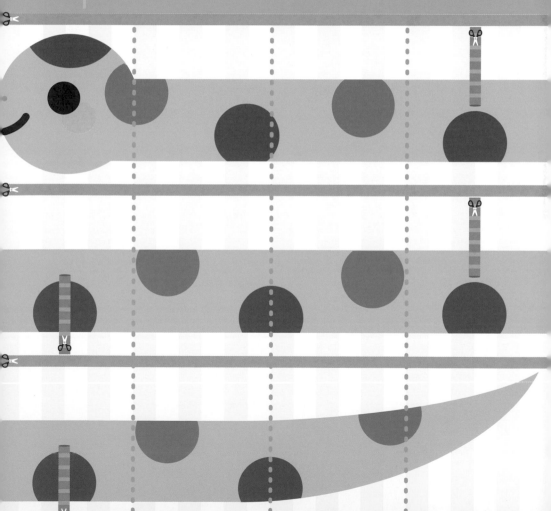

Slithering Snake

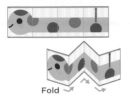

Fold

Fold the paper on the • • • • •
to make a wiggly snake.

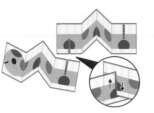

Insert one notch into another to
combine the pieces.

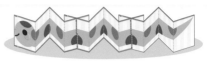

Make the slithering snake longer.

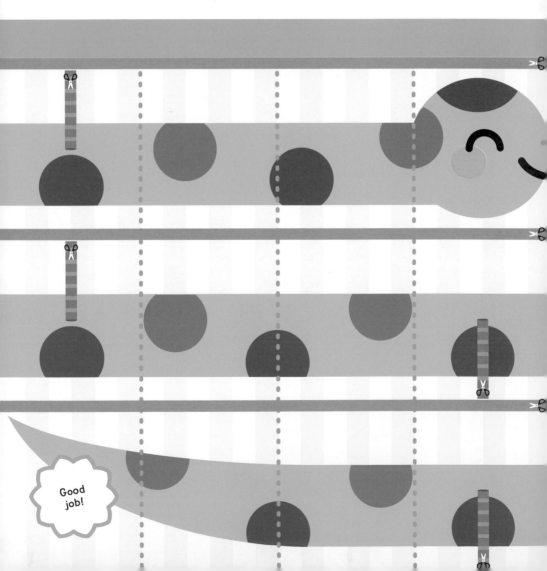

Good
job!

Fast Vehicles

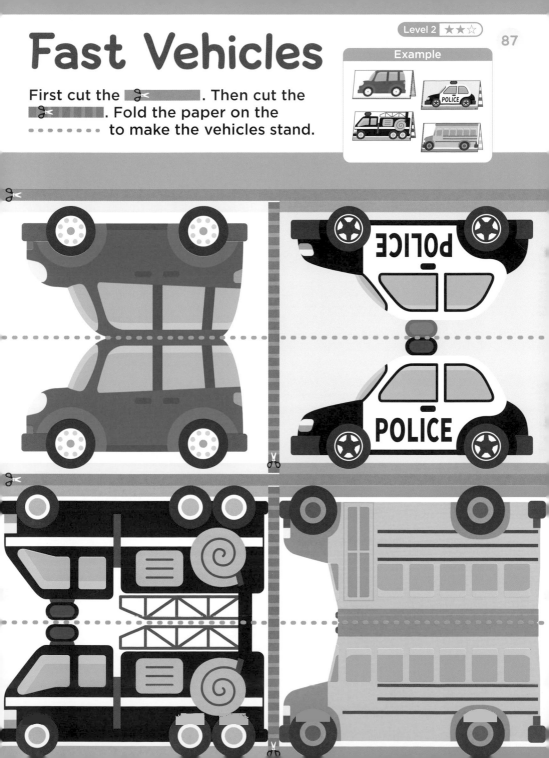

First cut the ✂▬▬▬. Then cut the
✂▬▬▬. Fold the paper on the
•••••••• to make the vehicles stand.

Example

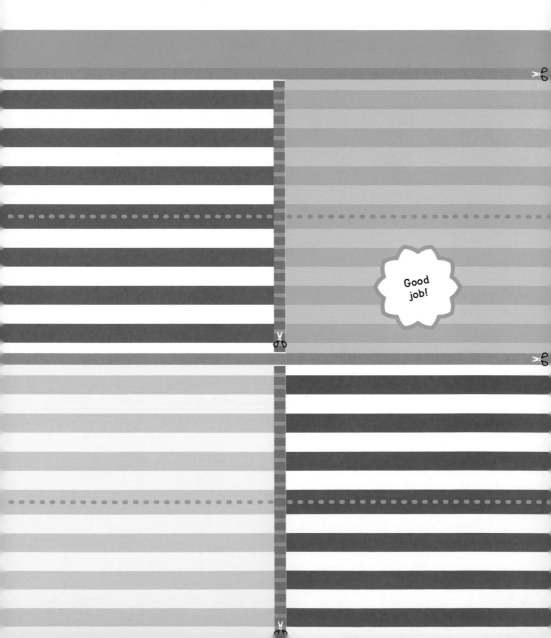

Good
job!

Zooming Airplane

Cut the ✂ ▬▬▬ .

Example

To Parents | If this is difficult for your child, roughly cut it out before giving it to them.

Good job!

Finger Puppets

Example

Back

Cut the ✂ ▓▓▓ first,
then the ✂ ▓▓▓ and
finally the ✂ ▓▓▓ .

☆See the back side of this page for
further instructions.

| To Parents | This activity practices cutting both straight and curved lines. After your child finishes cutting, have them fold the paper into a cylinder to make a finger puppet. |

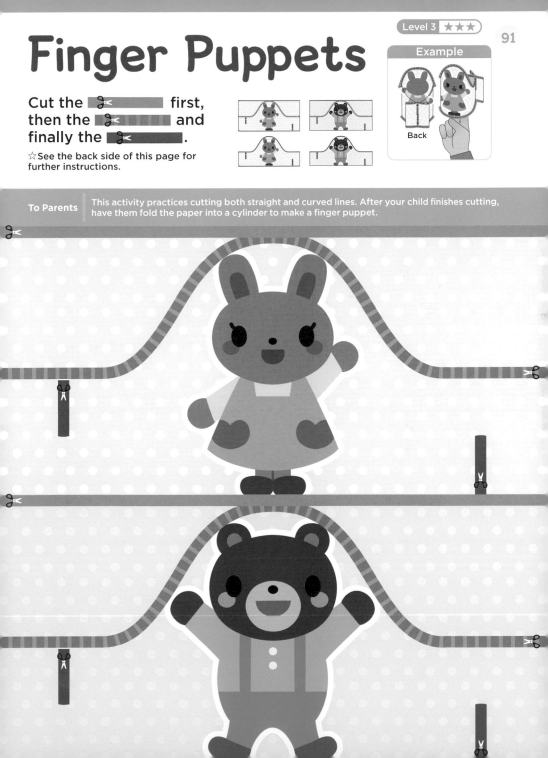

Finger Puppets

Cut along the ✂▬▬▬.

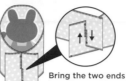

Stop here.

Bring the two ends together, and insert one notch into the other.

Play with your new finger puppet friend!

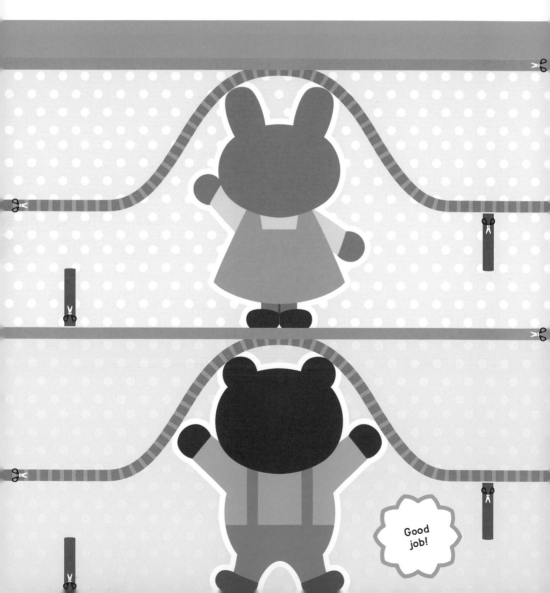

Good job!

Roller Coaster

Cut the ✂ ▓▓▓▓.

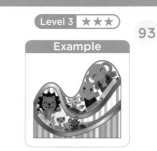

Good job!

Gliding Sailboat

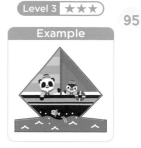

Example

Cut the ✂---------.

To Parents This yacht has many corners. Have your child cut while moving the position of the paper, not the scissors, when they need to change direction.

Ticking Clock

Example

Cut the .

Good job!

Floating Sea Otter

Example

Fold the paper on the ······· and attach the stickers.
Place the sticker on the back side of this page, then cut the ✂ .

Activity sticker

Floating Sea Otter

To Parents | This activity focuses on folding the paper and cutting while it's overlapped. When your child is finished, make the sea otter swing back and forth.

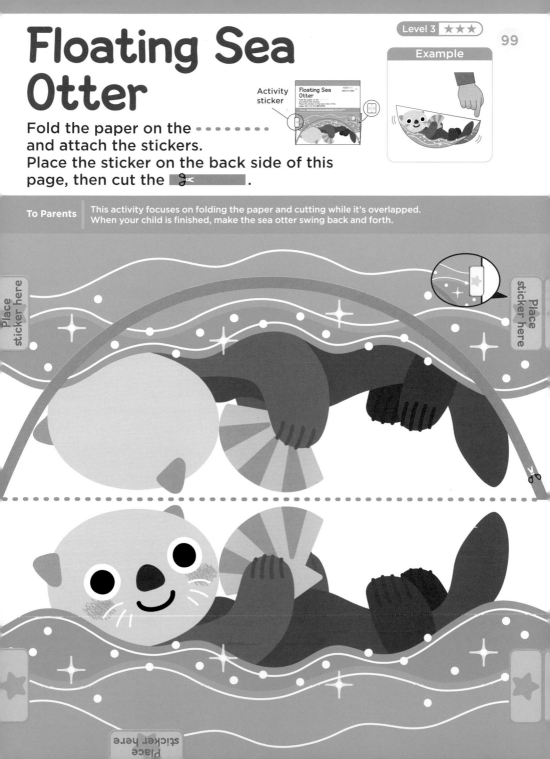

Place sticker here

Place sticker here

Place sticker here

Place sticker here

Floating Sea Otter

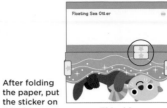

After folding the paper, put the sticker on this side.

This side

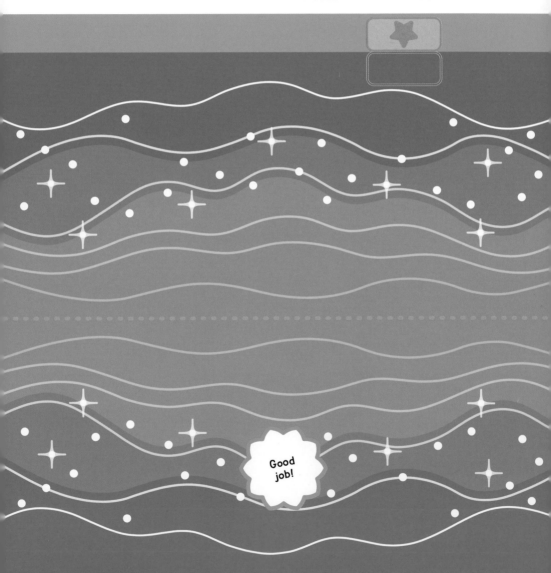

Good job!

Flying Balloon

Example

Fold the paper on the
• • • • • • • • • and attach the
stickers.
Cut the ✂ ▬▬▬▬.

Place sticker here

To Parents | Tell your child to fold, sticker, and cut in that order.

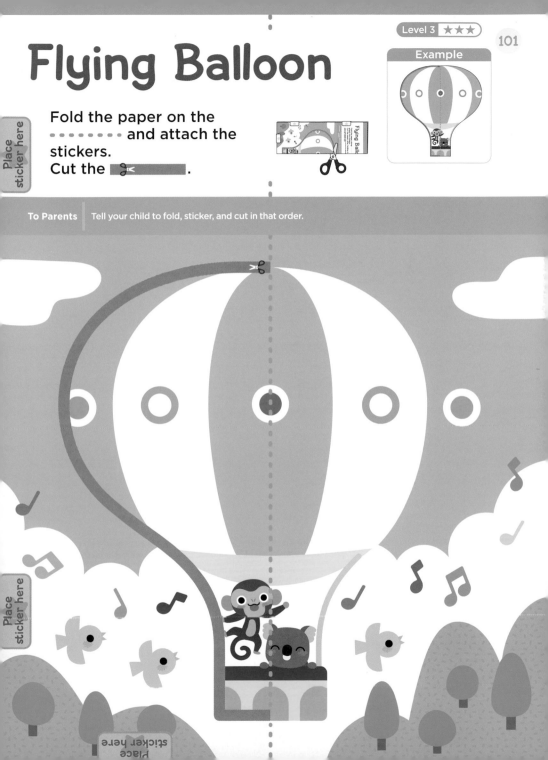

Place sticker here

Place sticker here

Flying Balloon

Ice Cream Swirl

Fold the paper on the • • • • • • • •
and attach the stickers.
Cut the ✂ ▬▬▬ .

Example

Ice Cream

Place sticker here

Place sticker here

Place sticker here

Birthday Cake

Example

Cut the .

Heart Card

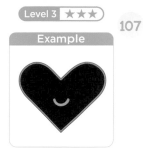

Cut the ✂ .

Yummy
Strawberry

Cut the .

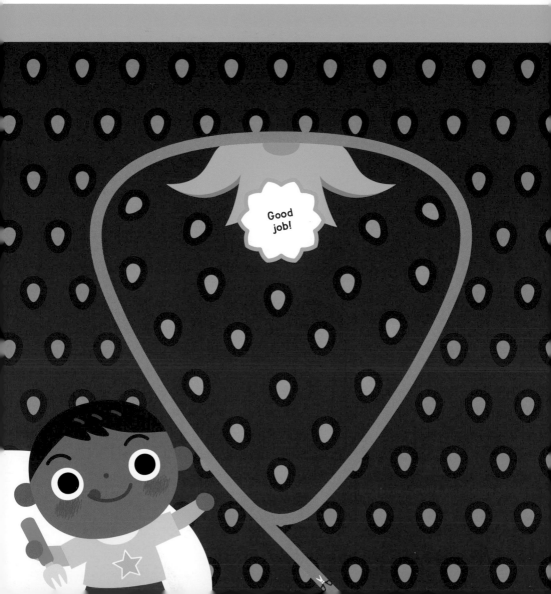

Sweet Bananas

Example

Cut the ✂ .

Flower Fairy

Cut the ✂ and pick up the Flower Fairy.

To Parents | Cutting a spiral line is similar to cutting a circle. Because the paper must be turned as your child cuts, encourage your child to move the position of the paper, not the scissors, as they go.

Soaring Rocket

Cut the ✂ and pick up the rocket.

To Parents Have your child rotate the paper, not the scissors, when the line changes direction, then continue cutting.

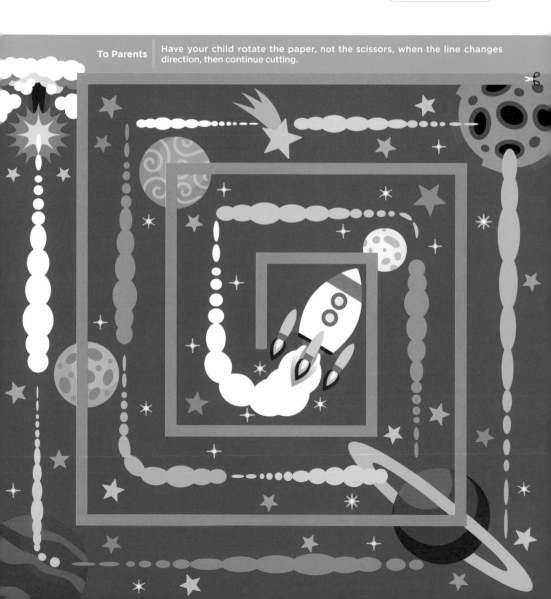

Good job!

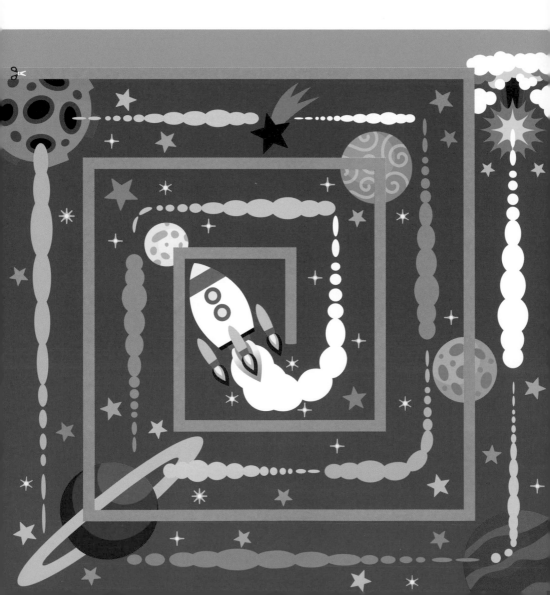

Spiral Snake

Cut the ✂ and pick up the snake.

To Parents | After your child cuts out the snake, pick up its head and shake it.

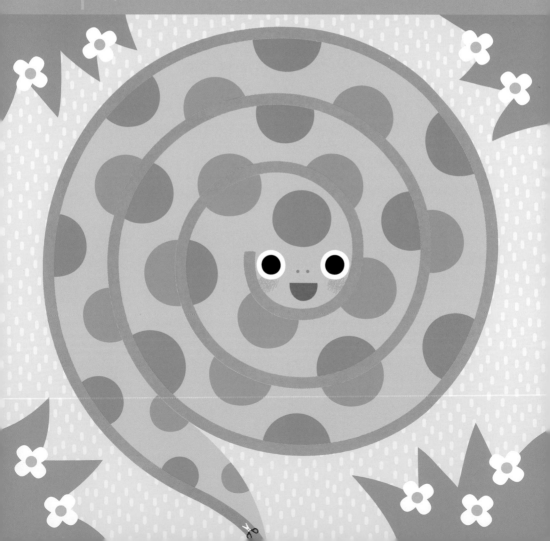

Good job!

Funny Panda

Cut the .

Example

To Parents Your child has successfully completed many activities throughout this book. They have practiced cutting and continue to improve. As your child cuts the panda's ears, have them cut while moving the position of the paper, not the scissors.

Fuzzy Cat

Cut the .

Beautiful Fish

Cut the  .

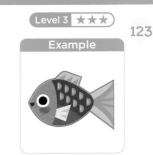

Beautiful Fish

Flying Bird

Example

Fold the paper on the • • • • • • • •
and attach the two sides together
with the stickers.
Also place the sticker on the back
side of this page, then cut the
✂— .

Sticker

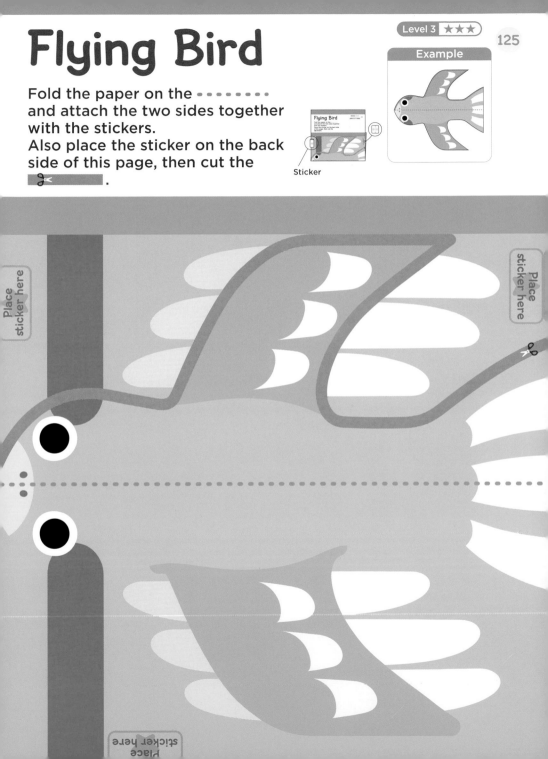

Place sticker here

Place sticker here

Place sticker here

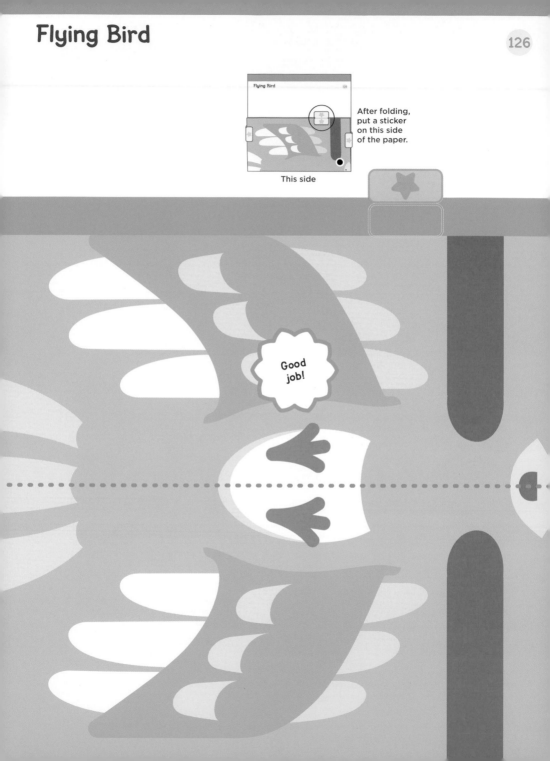

Talking Frog

Fold the paper along the
••••••••• and attach the sides
together with the stickers.
Cut the paper after folding it.

Example

To Parents | This is a complicated shape, but have your child cut, following the rule of moving the paper and not the scissors.

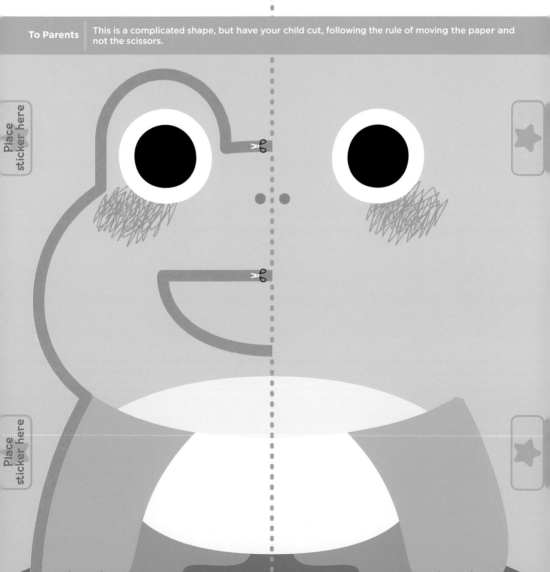

Place sticker here

Place sticker here

Hold the frog's cheeks.
Make it speak by opening
and closing its mouth.

Good
job!